H

Prayers

from

the

Journey

by

Juanita Ryan

©2013 Juanita Ryan

All rights reserved. No part of this book may be reproduced in any form without written permission from the author.

All Scripture quotations unless otherwise indicated are from the HOLY BIBLE, NEW INTERNATIONAL VERSION ©1973,1978,1984 by International Bible Society. Used by permission of Zondervan Publishing House. All rights reserved.

ISBN-13: 978-1484848258
ISBN-10: 148484825X

Printed in the United States of America

to Dale

Table of Contents

Introduction 7

Part I: Filtered Love

Desperate Prayer 10
Agnostic 11
All I Know 12
In Your Name 13
Dead End 14
Pursue Me 15
Half Sentences 16
Filtered Love 17
Pockets 18
At the Ocean 19
Give Me Peace 20
Artisan Hands 21
Your Child? 22
Give Me Grace 23
Surprise Party 24

Part 2: It's You I Want

You Carried Me 26
You Were There 27
It Is You I Want 28
Vulnerable One 29
You Hold Me 30
Joyful Servant 31
Mother God 32
Your Hand On Me 33
Re-membered 34
Your Suffering 35
Love's Power 36
This Is Me 37
I Was Blind But Now I See 38
Your Gaze 39
Sweet Comfort 40

Part 3: Open Spaces

How Silently 42
Our Father 43
I Am Yours 44
Naked 45
Washed Up 46
This Life 47
Gratitude 48
Quieted 49
You Are God, Calling Us 50
Today's Praise 51
Returning 52
First Thanks 53
The Ache of Missing 54
Perfectly Loved 55
Open Spaces 56

Part 4: Heaven at My Door

Your Will 58
Morning Prayer 59
True Love 60
Howling 61
Heaven At My Door 62
You Stay 63
Still You Stay 64
With You 65
It Is Good 66
Blessed Beauty 67
Altar of Praise 68
Receiving 69
Brilliant Dying 70
Small 71
Soaring 72

Afterword

Singing of Your Healing Love 74

Introduction

This volume is a collection of prayers written over several decades. They are prayers of distress and wonder, doubt and gratitude, pain and joy. At the time I wrote them, they were private expressions to God, not meant to be shared, except with a few people. But I have come to see that our encounters with God, and the ever deepening awakenings to God that can come from those encounters, are the best gifts given to us, and some of the most precious treasures we have to share. And so, I offer them to you as a crust of hope from the Bread of Heaven, that has feed and nourished me.

The first set of prayers come from the early years of my healing journey. It was a time when I was first coming to an end of trying harder, to an end of striving to earn some sense of worth, to an end of myself. It was a time brimming with pain, doubts, fears and hesitant first-steps of learning the true meaning of ancient words like "trust" and "love."

The second set of prayers speak of gifts of healing. They reflect encounters with Jesus, experiences of being held safe in the midst of great danger, moments of knowing myself as the much loved child we all are and stirrings of my deepest longings for my heart's true Home. The third and fourth sets of prayers are expressions of some of the ebb and flow of the ongoing awakenings, regular struggles, deepening surrenders, growing trust, quiet interludes, continued healing and overflowing gratitude that are a part of this ongoing journey.

Wherever you are on your journey, I pray that some of what you read here will help you find your own voice to sing out your fears and grief, your longings and joy, your gratitude and awe to the One who knows you fully and treasures you deeply.

I pray that you will experience some sense of companionship in these pages—some sense of meeting a fellow struggler who wishes you well and wants you to know that wherever you find yourself on this road, God is with you—offering to guide and love you with a love that is unshakable, powerful and tender.

Part 1

Filtered Love

Desperate Prayer

A single
silent
scream
launches
with
sudden
violence
from
my inner
depths
and
rockets
toward
the distant
steel
blue
sky.
And for
just
an instant
I can
see
white
jet stream
forming
a vapor
link
between
my stricken
heart
and
you.

I will not keep silent;
I will speak out in the anguish of my spirit.

Job 7:11

Agnostic

I feel as if
I do not know you
anymore.
I am agnostic.

In this place
of not knowing,
I sit and wait,
wondering
if you really are,
and if all I ever dared
hope about you
and your love
can possibly be true.

You claim
to show yourself
to people like me.
All I can do is look for you
and wait for you.

But how long?
How long?

How long, O Lord?
Will your forget
me forever?
How long will you hide your face from me?
How long must I wrestle with my thoughts
and every day have sorrow in my heart?

Psalm 13:1-2

All I Know

All the complex considerations
of doctrines,
all the debate over
interpretations,
are like a faint and distant roar
to my weary heart.

I have no strength
to entertain such matters.
I have been stripped
of my presuming.
All I have left
is one sure and simple thing.

It is this.
I need you.
This is the sum total
of my faith today.
It is my one sentence
doctrinal statement.

It is all I know.
But I know it
from the depths of my being.
I need you.

I need you.

Yet I am poor and needy;
may the Lord think of me.

Psalm 40:17

In Your Name

I am tired of pretending
in your name.
I am tired of pretending
that problems don't exist,
that feelings are
to be disregarded.
I am tired of pretending
that I do not struggle.

I need truth, not pretense.
I am hungry for what is real.
I long to feel passionately
the joy
and sorrow
you made me capable of.

I need,
in your name,
to weep and to laugh,
to mourn and to dance.
I need to experience
the richness
of all you made me
capable of feeling.
I need to experience it all
in your name.

*There is a time for everything,
and a season for every activity under heaven;
a time to weep
and a time to laugh,
a time to mourn
and a time to dance.*

Ecclesiastes 3: 1,4

Dead End

I have came to a dead end.
The path I journeyed for years
has came to a sudden stop
at the edge of a cliff.

Exhausted and numb, I sit
dangling my feet over the brink.
Alone. Bewildered.
Stunned that my efforts
have lead to this.

My mind has lost all sense
of confidence and strength.
"I don't know," was my last sigh.

And so, I sit.
Silent. Waiting. Undone.

I ask, now,
emptied and ready to listen,
for your wisdom.
What now? What is your way?
My way has come to an end.

If any of you lacks wisdom,
he should ask God,
who gives generously
to all without finding fault,
and it will be given to him.

James 1:5

Pursue Me

Pursue me.
Break through my defenses.
Come crashing through
these internal walls
that hide me from you.
I long to fall into
your loving arms.
But I cannot
find my way
through this maze
of fear.
Come.
Find me.
Set me free.

*The Spirit of the Lord is on me...he has sent me
to proclaim freedom for the prisoners.*

Luke 4: 16-18

Half Sentences

My prayers are
half sentences today.
Chopped up thoughts,
hesitant bits of conversation,
spill from my fearful heart.

It hurts too much
to say it all,
to think it through,
to feel in one lump sum.

Take these incomplete
fragments,
pearls of pain,
string them together
on the enduring thread
of your love.

Make a necklace
of my heart's
half spoken cries.

Give ear to my words, O Lord,
consider my sighing.
Listen to my cry for help,
my King and my God,
for to you I pray.

Psalm 5:1-2

Filtered Love

I would not be able to bear
your piercing pure love
if you should show yourself
to me directly.

You seem to know this
and so filter
the blazing light of your kindness
through human voices
and flower faces.

A friend's concern,
a child's laugh,
a sparrow's song
are the muted tones
and shaded light you use
to touch me.

Your filtered presence is building
a growing hope in me
that love might be a possibility.

Thank you
for all the gentle ways
you reach me.

They did not realize it was I who healed them.
I led them with
cords of human kindness,
with ties of love;
I lifted the yoke from their neck
and bent down to feed them.

Hosea 11: 3b-4

Pockets

I don't have
a proper pocket;
none large enough
to carry
your kindness
and respect.
Your generous gifts
slip awkwardly
from my hands
as I fumble for a place
to keep them.
I need to
sew me some
way-down-deep-pockets,
big enough
to hold your love.

For this reason I kneel before the Father.
And I pray that you,
being rooted and established
in love, may have power... to know this love
that surpasses knowledge—
that you may be filled to the measure
of all the fullness of God.

Ephesians 3:14,17,19

At the Ocean

We sat beside your
wild, wet skirt,
wanting to soothe our sore hearts
by watching your joyful jig.

But we were too absorbed
in our pain
to gain perspective
from your frolicking.

We talked
and sighed,
sitting there on that smooth rock
beside your playful splendor.

Until you picked up
a corner of your hem
and splashed us
wet, salty and surprised.

Play! Laugh! Enjoy!
you called as you pulled
your skirt away.
You gently splashed us
into an unexpected state of silly.

And, so, we laughed
and inadvertently let ourselves
feel something bigger
and better
than our problems.
We felt you.

*Gladness and joy will overtake them,
and sighing and sorrow will flee away.*

Isaiah 51:11

Give Me Peace

Give me peace,
not a hopeless resignation,
giving into the darkness,
but a growing certainty that
one day Light will dawn.

Give me peace,
not a deadening novocain
that robs outrage,
but a quiet awareness of Presence
in the angst of the day.

Give me peace,
not a passionless state
of not-seeing, not knowing,
but a fierce, calm clarity
about what matters most.

Give me peace,
not a smugness or pretense,
but an internal sense of being held
that allows me to live as outrageously
as one who is loved might live.

*Peace I leave with you;
my peace I give you.*

John 14:27

Artisan Hands

Hold me gently
in your strong, artisan hands
as you pressure, push, pull,
remake me.
Hold me securely
as the life wheel
spins beneath my frame
in cycles of birth,
death,
rebirth.
Hold me faithfully
as you make
sturdy, solid,
hard-as-diamond
those brittle, broken places
and soft, molten
liquid-as-pure-gold
those places that need to learn
to yield
in graceful vulnerability.

Yet, O Lord, you are our Father.
We are the clay, you are the potter;
we are all the work of your hand.

Isaiah 64:8

Your Child?

You invite me to be your child.
An overture I have often declined
since the thought of childhood frightens me.

But I am beginning to wonder
if you are offering me
an experience of childhood
as it was meant to be.

Maybe you are saying
that with you I can enjoy
unselfconscious wonder,
because you will share in my delight.

That, with you, I can be unabashedly dependent
because you will welcome hearing
and responding to my needs.

That with you I can spontaneously express all my feelings, because you care about me.

That with you I can always be learning
 and questioning, because you will patiently,
joyfully teach me.

You call me your child,
inviting me to be the child
I never had an opportunity to be,
offering me a second chance
at growing up loved.

I am amazed. Grateful. Ready.

*How great is the love the Father has lavished on us,
that we should be called children of God!*

I John 3:1

Give Me the Grace

Give me the grace
to care
without neglecting my needs,

the humility
to assist
without rescuing,

the kindness
to be clear
without being cold,

the mercy
to be angry
without rejecting,

the prudence
to disclose
without disrespecting my privacy,

the humor
to admit human failings
without experiencing shame,

the compassion
to give freely, fully,
without selfish ambition or pride.

In your anger do not sin...
Be kind and compassionate to one another,

Ephesians 4: 26,32

Surprise Party

You came running up behind me
and jumped up on my back,
asking for a ride and
laughing in my ear.
Out of nowhere
you ambushed me
and left me suddenly smiling.

My feet that had been dragging
suddenly are dancing.

This is no quiet, somber
thoughtful joy.
It is a foot-stomping
knee-slapping
raucous joy.

I never dreamed that joy
would catch up to me.

You have given me a surprise party.

Thank you.

*You fill me with joy
in your presence.*

Psalm 16:11

Part 2

It's You I Want

You Carried Me

You swaddled me
in white robed arms,
rescued me
from my dark terror.
I carried pain,
but you carried me
away
and up,
up into the light,
until I burst
into a thousand
splintered rays
of joy.

I have made you and I will carry you;
I will sustain you and I will rescue you.

Isaiah 46:4

You Were There

Quivering I stared
into the black abyss
until I felt you nudge me
to let go
and slip
over the edge.
I found myself
floating in that darkness
held and filled with energy
so sweet and strong
it could only be you.
Your voice came to me
rich and playful,
"Child, did you really think
there could be anywhere
that I am not?"

Where can I go from your Spirit?
Where can I flee from your presence?
If I go up to the heavens, you are there;
if I make my bed in the depths,
you are there.

Psalm 139: 7-8

It Is You I Want

It is you I want
        Love I came from,
        Love that made me.
Ah, to return
to your heart's vast ocean,
        where I lose myself,
        and find myself,
        and lose myself again.

As the deer pants for streams of water,
so my soul pants for you, O God.
My soul thirsts for God, for the living God.

Psalm 42:1

You Hold Me

You hold me gently,
allowing me to be a child.
Allowing me to not understand,
to say "it is too hard for me."
Allowing me to say
"I need you" all the time.

You hold me securely,
allowing me to be a child.
Allowing me to love you—
sweet innocence restored.
Allowing me to feel
myself tenderly loved by you.

You hold me always,
allowing me to be a child.
Allowing me to be alive, playful,
stilled, quieted.
Allowing me to rest,
knowing in your arms
all is well.

"Let the little children come to me, and do not hinder them
for the kingdom of God belongs to such as these.
I tell you the truth, anyone who will not receive
the kingdom of God
like a little child will never enter it."
And he took the children in his arms,
put his hands on them and blessed them.

Mark 10: 14-16

Vulnerable One

You, God,
are the vulnerable One.
I am creature, child.
Yet my heart is rock hard in places.
While your heart—
your heart is
liquid love
and longing.
You hold nothing back.

How often I have longed to gather your children together,
as a hen gathers her chicks under her wings
but you would not..

Matthew 23:37

Joyful Servant

I sat alone,
thinking about you
when I sensed you
kneeling in front of me.

My response was like Peter's:
"Lord, it is I who should..."
but I saw the joy on your face.

Jesus, you are divine,
yet you call yourself
my brother
and kneel before me,
a Joyful Servant.
I want to receive
this gift from you.

Jesus, I want be like you.
Teach me to kneel
in joy with you
before all others.

When he had finished washing their feet,
he put on his clothes and returned to his place.
"Do you understand what I have done for you?"
he asked them. "Now that I, your Lord and Teacher,
have washed your feet,
you also should wash one another's feet."

John 13: 12-14

Mother God

"I am your Mother"

Your words fell like sweet rain
into the barren caverns
of my motherless grief.

"I am the One who gave you life;
who sustains you.
I am the One who feeds you,
who comforts you, who nurtures you.
I am the One who loves you
and who has always loved you.
I am your Mother."

Mother God?
Help me.
I do not know you this way.
Mother.
God.

*Can a mother forget the baby at her breast
and have no compassion on the child she has borne?
Though she may forget, I will not forget you!*

Isaiah 49:14-16

Your Hand On Me

Sometimes I feel
your hand on me,
resting on my shoulder
while I sit at my work,
or on my head
as I fall asleep.
I love your hand on me.
You comfort me
with your presence.
You center me in your love.
You strengthen me
with your joy.
I love your hand on me.

*Because you are my help,
I sing in the shadow of your wings.
My soul clings to you,
your right hand upholds me.*

Psalm 63:7-8

Re-membered

You knelt beside me
in my times of darkness
pouring Yourself—
Love, Life—
into me.

I had thought you left me,
but you did not.

When the time came
for me to re-member
the darkness,
you allowed me to
re-member you as well.
You knelt beside me
and your love—
brighter than all the darkness—
filled me.

*Arise, shine, for your light has come,
and the glory of the Lord rises upon you.*

Isaiah 60:1

Your Suffering

You brought me to your cross,
to your suffering.
I felt your love even then,
poured out for us all.
I wept,
I knelt,
I stood,
I called to you.
My only thought was
to comfort you,
to let you know I was there,
to tell you that I love you.

I stayed
until the vision faded
and you spoke:

"This is how I was with you
in your suffering—
holding you,
loving you,
protecting the deepest
parts of you.
Your love for me
in my suffering
is a glimpse of my love for you
in your suffering.
Trust this love.
Live in this love.
Let this love live in you."

*When they came to the place called the Skull,
there they crucified him.*

Luke 23:33

Love's Power

You showed me the palm
of your luminous hand—
your hand of mercy
and kindness,
your hand of love
and blessing.
On the outer corner there was
a dark speck.
"This speck represents
all the evil of all time
gathered together,"
you told me.
"The darkness,
that can seem to blot out
all light at times,
is but a speck
compared to the vastness and
strength of my love.
And even this speck will
one day
be no more.
Trust the beauty
and strength
of my love,
it will endure forever.

I will sing of the Lord's great love forever;
with my mouth I will make your faithfulness
known through all generations.
I will declare that your love stands firm forever,
that you established your faithfulness in heaven itself.
O Lord God Almighty, who is like you?
You are mighty, O Lord,
and your faithfulness surrounds you.

Psalm 89:1-2,8

This Is Me

You stood with me
as I looked at myself through time.
A small child,
carrying great pain.
I did not want to acknowledge
the child
or the pain,
Yet I knew you were
inviting me to do so.

"This is not me.
This suffering cannot be mine,"
I said.

You responded,
surprising me again.
"This is me. This suffering is mine."

You are so fully with me,
you are so much a part of me,
that all my sorrow
and all my joy
are yours as well?

In your tender strength
I found the courage and humility
to at last embrace
this suffering child.

"This is me," I wept.

*Surely he took up our infirmities
and carried our sorrows,*

Isaiah 53:4

I Was Blind But Now I See

I sat holding myself as a child.
Yet not a child at all,
but a monster,
unrecognizable as human.

You came, Jesus,
and stretched out your hand.
"Ah," I thought,
"You will heal this child."

I looked at you,
your hand reaching,
your eyes twinkling.
You were an artist at play.

But your hand did not
touch the monster child.

Instead, you touched
my adult eyes
so I could see.
So I could see this
one on my lap clearly.
Not as the monster
my fears and shame imagined,
but as the simple,
sweet,
innocent
child
I am.

One thing I do know,
I was blind, but now I see.

John 9:25

Your Gaze

You gazed at me,
inviting me to gaze back
into the ocean of your love.
It was unbearable.
I could not sustain a gaze.
Only glances.

Your love
fell in waves
against my shame and fear and pride,
carrying away small segments a little at a time.
It felt like certain death.
And so it was.

Little by little I died.
I thought there would be nothing left.
But you knew the seed of life
you had once formed in me
would lie exposed,
aching with love and longing.
And so I was.

I was unearthed
by your loving gaze.
You treated me
as though I were the pearl of great price
that you had sold everything to buy.
And so you had.

The kingdom of heaven is like a treasure hidden in a field.
When a man found it, he hid it again,
and then in his joy went and sold all he had
and bought the field.

Matthew 13:44

Sweet Comfort

We sit together,
near the water's edge.
Your arm of protection
around me,
my head resting
near your heart.

When the waters
lap lazy,
I am able, at times,
to quiet my mind
and relax into your
steady
embrace.

But when waves
of fear rise up
like threatening armies
and explode at our feet,
I too often loose all
bearings
and forget that you are
there.

I practice being brave,
as I learned in child-
hood, and steel myself
against these rising hosts,
only to find myself
trembling.

Teach me that all I need
to do is bury my face in
your chest and speak my
fear, my need, into all the
love and strength
you are.

Teach me,
so I might remember
and receive again
the deep peace
your sweet comfort
always brings.

Do not be anxious about anything, but in every situation,
by prayer and petition, with thanksgiving,
present your requests to God.
And the peace of God, which transcends all understanding,
will guard your hearts and your minds in Christ Jesus.

Philippians 4: 6-7

Part 3

Open Spaces

How Silently

Like a slight breeze
stirring a lace curtain at an open window,

like a blue winged dragonfly
setting off a single ripple across a still lake,

like a first snow fall
descending soft, hushing all,

so you are with us,
achingly gentle
in your touch, your voice, your presence
moving in us,
awakening us to you.

Because of the tender mercies of our God…
the rising sun will come to us from heaven.

Luke 1:78

Our Father

We are your children.

May we know you as
our true and loving Father,
Merciful One,
Compassionate One.

Thank you that you are here
with us and in us, actively
working to heal and free and
bless us.

May we receive you. May we
say "Yes" to you and to your
loving will for us. May we
participate with you in your
healing, restoring work,
in our lives, in our families,
in our communities, in our
world.

Thank you that every day you
feed us, you nurture us. You
give us all we need, one day at
a time.

We confess that we fall short.
We harden our hearts in pride
and despair, in greed and
disregard of others, and yet,
you forgive us and release us,
and call us, always, to learn
your way of love.

May we, in response to your
kindness, extend mercy and
forgiveness to all others. We
ask you to protect us from the
ever present temptation to see
ourselves in competition with
others for your love, when
you love us all, always.

Free us, as well, from the fear
that we can be separated from
your love.

May we know you always
present to us all,
Most Powerful,
Most Beautiful God.

Our Father which art in heaven, Hallowed be thy name.

Luke 11:2

I Am Yours

You made me.
I am yours.
I came from you.
Your life and light are in me.
Free every cell of my body,
every part of my being
to know this,
to celebrate this,
to live this,
to dance in joy.

It is he who made us, and we are his.

Psalm 100:3

Naked

It is so excruciating
and messy,
so sacred
and wondrous,
this peeling away
of all we hold onto,
all we hide behind,
until the naked,
beautiful soul
we are
is exposed
and your light
and life in us
shines through.

*"You are the light of the world.
A town built on a hill cannot be hidden.
Neither do people light a lamp and put it under a bowl.
Instead they put it on its stand,
and it gives light to everyone in the house.*

Matthew 5:14-15

Washed Up

You ask to wash my feet,
as you disrobe and
kneel before me.
You wait, looking up at me.
Joy dances in your eyes.
I cannot breathe.
Everything in me threatens
to break loose, melt, flow,
in the warmth of such tenderness.
Your kindness undoes me.
Your naked love disarms me,
inviting me to bare all, too.
If I say yes,
the great flood of my longing,
my need, my pure joy
will break me open.
Yes.
I say, yes.
Please. Wash me.

Jesus knew that the Father had put all things under his power, and that he had come from God and was returning to God; so he got up from the meal, took off his outer clothing, and wrapped a towel around his waist. After that, he poured water into a basin and began to wash his disciples' feet, drying them with the towel that was wrapped around him.

John 13: 3-5

This Life

This life I claim as mine,
hold onto
and defend,
is a gift,
entrusted for a time,
given, breath-by-breath
by you.

It is a vessel
carved rough
and beautiful
for you
to pour yourself into
and overflow from,
for your joy
and mine
and others.

It is a gift I cannot
truly receive,
you whisper repeatedly,
until I release my grip
and let it go to you.
Help me
as I open hands and heart
to release
and receive
your gift again.

For whoever wants to save his life will lose it,
but whoever loses his life for me will save it.

Luke 9:24

Gratitude

"Thank you. Thank you," she'd say,
offering her soft spoken hymn of praise to you
with each step she took.
Ninety seven, clutching walker,
while I held onto her,
she walked in thankful wonder
like a toddler taking first steps with glee.
Each step a gift, counted.
Walker steadied and grounded her body in motion
while her thanksgiving steadied and grounded her spirit
in the here and now flow of grace.

I lost count of how many of these short walks we took
that last sweet year of her life,
saying our thank yous to you out loud
down the hall and back.
But they were many and enough to echo in my cells
and to raise up in me from time to time
this simple hymn of praise.

"Thank you. Thank you."
I find myself whispering to you
over and over throughout the day,
noticing how my eyes open to the outpouring
of grace and blessing in every moment,
how I feel myself carried in the current of your joy,
how I am able to use this walker of gratitude
to steady and ground heart and mind, body and soul
in your glorious presence with us here and now.

Thank you. Thank you.

*I will praise God's name in song and
glorify him with thanksgiving.*

Psalm 69:30

Quieted

You quieted me.
I came to you with fears,
finally willing
to acknowledge them to myself
so I could speak them to you.
How you comfort me.
How gently you receive me.
How sweetly you remind me
of your Presence,
drawing me into that still center
where I am free to simply be,
where I rest in your goodness,
your greatness,
your love,
where I know, again,
that you are God.

*Be still and know
that I am God.*

Psalm 46:10

You are God, Calling Us

As seas rise, and island nations disappear,
causing our hope to crumble,
you are God.

As drought leaves earth barren and rock hard,
matching our despairing hearts,
you are God.

As mighty winds rip and endless rains destroy,
tearing at the fabric of our trust,
you are God.

As corrupt powers rule and oppress the weak,
crushing our spirits,
you are God.

As violence abounds and wars persist,
darkening our world, our lives,
you are God.

You are God,
calling us to hope in your goodness,
calling us to trust in your power,
calling us to know peace in your presence.

You are God,
calling us to care for the earth and for each other,
calling us to do what is fair and just,
calling us to act in kindness and mercy.

You are God,
calling us to bless both friend and enemy,
calling us to be healers and burden bearers,
calling us to love like you love.

God is our refuge and strength, an ever-present help in trouble.

Psalm 46:1-3, 9-10

Today's Praise

Thank you for palm trees
swaying,
fountain flowing,
ocean breezes blowing,
out the window as I hear
I am five years, cancer free.

Thank you for three year old
singing,
nine year old fishing,
nearby family visiting,
in this new community
that is becoming their own.

Thank you for grace while
waiting,
loan finally closing,
keys soon opening
the blessed place
he will now call home.

Thank you for friends
supporting,
spouse holding,
your presence abiding,
in sickness and in health
and through each new
season of life.

Praise the Lord, my soul;
all my inmost being, praise his holy name.

Psalm 103:1

Returning

Skin and muscle
have come loose from their
moorings
starting their descent
back to earth's
dark
womb.

While spirit raises
joyful child arms
heaven ward
stretching with
awe and wonder
toward
your
loving
light.

*Even to your old age and gray hairs
I am he, I am he who sustains you.
I have made you and I will carry you,
I will sustain you and I will rescue you.*

Isaiah 46:4

First Thanks

For early morning light coming in sideways,
waking day lilies,
for neon-blue-breasted hummingbird,
feeding on golden hibiscus,
for towering maple,
laden with summer's deep green foliage,
thank you.

For breezes playing wind chimes and cooling skin,
for violin concerto
in the flight of the fly,
for quiet delighting with you
at the start of this new day,
thank you.

Delight yourself in the Lord.

Psalm 37:4

The Ache of Missing

I feel the downward pull,
the pout brewing,
the demands building,
wanting to hang onto
what was never mine.

I watch as this happens.
How I let go and let go
only to want to grasp again
in selfish greed
that would wound us all.

Grant me strength
to stay with the ache of missing.
Grant me the trust of a small child
to bow to your will and way
in this season of separation.

Remind me, that although there is pain
in each surrender,
it is this emptying
that makes room
for your gifts
and for you.

Love is patient, love is kind.
It does not envy, it does not boast,
it is not proud. It does not dishonor others,
it is not self-seeking.

I Corinthians 13:4-7

Perfectly Loved

"I know things aren't perfect,"
she said as an aside,
judging the imperfections she observed
by harsh standards she
holds herself and others to.

The wonder, that I noticed
with quiet celebration, Lord,
was my ability to embrace this truth
with gratitude.

Not perfect. Yes.
But no shame. Only quiet joy.
Messy. Healing still.
Not perfect.

Yet perfectly loved by you.
And resting in this,
the deepest of all truths.
Such grace that you have taught me this.
Such. Amazing. Grace.

Be merciful, just as your Father is merciful.
Do not judge, and you will not be judged.
Do not condemn, and you will not be condemned.
Forgive, and you will be forgiven.

Luke 6:36, 37

Open Spaces

The land stretches far,
moving beyond horizons on every side,
lying flat, receptive, beneath the great sky.

Broken open by farmers' plow
prepared to drink in rain and sun
and yield the staff of life.

We call these vast open spaces, these majestic plains,
the Heartland.

And I think, as I fly above them in my mind's eye,
how life's changes and challenges stretch me.
And how you offer
to use such moments,
to create new, open spaces in my heartland.

Offering as well,
to farm and husband this new land,
breaking open hardened places.

You, always desiring to make me ready
to receive more fully the richness of your life.

You, Farmer,
eager to plant and harvest spiritual food,
in my heartland, to feed the hungry soul.

Jesus… told this parable: "A farmer went out to sow his seed. As he was scattering the seed, some fell along the path; it was trampled on, and the birds ate it up. Some fell on rocky ground, and when it came up, the plants withered because they had no moisture. Other seed fell among thorns, which grew up with it and choked the plants. Still other seed fell on good soil. It came up and yielded a crop, a hundred times more than was sown."

Luke 8:4-8

Part 4

Heaven at My Door

Your Will

The familiar words
spill off the page,
falling onto my lap.
What? Really?
Joy is your will for me?

It sounds like
pollyanna pretense.
It is not how I imagine
your will to be,
I protest, scooping the
words into my hands.

Continual joy,
prayer and thanksgiving?
I hold the words up to you
because I cannot do this,
your will,
without your help.
Please, show me how.

And so you do, opening
the eyes of my heart.
I see and feel myself, to my
surprise, a child,
holding your hand,
skipping along in sheer
delight, so happy just to be
with you.

You took the words
I held out to you
and gave me back
a tender image,
a visceral picture
of your meaning.

This is your will,
your invitation to us.
This is life as you designed
it to be. Just this.
Thankful, joyful
to be with you,
holding your hand,
walking,
skipping at your side.

Constant joy is
being with you.
Continual prayer,
our hand in yours.
Ready to give thanks
in all circumstances,
because
in all circumstances,
you are there.

Be joyful always. Pray constantly.
Give thanks in all circumstances.
For this is God's will for you, in Christ Jesus.

I Thessalonians 5: 16-19

Morning Prayer

I give my mind, my heart,
my body, my spirit,
my day, my life,
to you.
For all I am
and all I have
is from you.
All are gifts,
that I return
in gratitude and love to you.
To you, Self-giving God,
who gives all you are
to me and to us all.
To you, whose life and love
were poured out to us in Christ.
To you who comes to us,
ever so intimately as Spirit,
to dwell with us, in us.
To you who draws us
always deeper into
your Father's heart
of goodness and love.
Receive the gift
of all I am and have,
I pray.
Free me to receive
the fullness of
the gift of you,
today.

Every good and perfect gift is from above,
coming down from the Father of the heavenly lights,
who does not change like shifting shadows.

James 1:17

True Love

You call me
a name unimagined,
raising me up
from the place
I have fallen.

"My beautiful one, rise,"
you say, as you lift me with
graceful motion
into your embrace.

"The rains have stopped.
The winter is over.
The season of singing has
begun. Come, let me show
you what winter's deaths
have birthed."

You, True Love,
come to us all in this way,
naming our beauty,
reaching to lift us
with grace from the place
of our falling
into the heaven
of your arms.
You whisper hope
to our souls
of bird song and blossoms,
of spreading vines
and greening woods,
of sweet fruit ripening,
of new life, replacing
winter's death.

You name us anew, raise
us, embrace us, awaken our
senses, invite us to come
with you.

May we, shaken
with wonder,
breathe in your love,
be strengthened,
made ready, to sing our
glad hallelujahs.

My lover spoke and said to me,
Arise, my darling,
my beautiful one, and come with me.
See! The winter is past; the rains are over and gone.
Flowers appear on the earth;
the season of singing has come,
the cooing of doves is heard in our land.
The fig tree forms its early fruit;
the blossoming vines spread their fragrance.
Arise, come, my darling;
my beautiful one, come with me.

Song of Songs 2:9-13

Howling

We howled happiness
sitting together
in the gentle
morning light.
It was no joke,
only delicious delight
in each other
and living gratitude
for so much grace,
that sent us silly.

Later, when I was
still and listening,
you took me back
to those shared moments
of holy howling
to let me look again
into this loved one's eyes,
and hear anew our glad
sounds.

"You caught a glimpse
of me in those joy filled
eyes," you said.

"You witnessed the truth
of how I see you.
You can hear in your
hilarious howls
an echo of my voice,
for I howl in happiness
over you."

"Your deepening delight
in each other
and in me
is response and reflection
of my celebration of you."

"Howl happiness often.
Live glorious gratitude
every day.
Let your joy be full.
It is my joy you share."

If you keep my commands, you will remain in my love,
just as I have kept my Father's commands
and remain in his love.
I have told you this so that my joy may be in you
and that your joy may be complete.
My command is this:
Love each other as I have loved you.

John 15: 10-12

Heaven at My Door

I hear you
tapping gently,
but oh, so persistently.
Your morse code
of desire
moves in waves
from the door
to the inner chambers
of my being.

It seems you are
always there,
vulnerably offering
your self,
your love,
your goodness.

Heaven is standing
at my door,
seeking entrance
and I hesitate.
Love is offering me
everything
and I question
my deserving.

Some ancient fear
has chained
the door again,
allowing me
to crack it open
just enough
to let the light
of your beauty stream in.

What fear bars
my way to you?
What healing
do you bring
to me with this new
awakening?

Show me, Lord.
Though I weep
as if I will die,
undo the chain
of this fear.
And come in.

Here I am! I stand at the door and knock. If anyone hears my voice and opens the door, I will come in and eat with that person, and they with me.

Revelation 3:20

You Stay

"You stayed with me.
You stayed with me."
I turn this truth over quietly,
letting it calm me,
like a cool, smooth
worry stone in my hand.

You stayed with me
when the person I needed most
turned away, walked away, left.
You stayed.
Every time.
You stayed.

This reality, a gift
you spoke into my heart's darkness,
grows more solid—
becoming an intimate stone of comfort—
as I touch and turn it over
again and again.

I hold it gently
until it takes hold of me,
and forms new circuits
on which to send
the healing Light of your Presence
into crevices of untouched pain.

You stayed.
You stay.
You are the One
who always stays with me.

God has said, "Never will I leave you; never will I forsake you."

Hebrews 13:5

Still You Stay

You stay with me
even when I do not stay,
even when I turn away,
walk away
from myself.
You stay with me,
though left for dead,
abandoned.

You stay,
weeping
beside my
self imposed tomb,
call out my name,
awaken me from death
to life with you.

You stay with me
even when I turn away,
walk away
from others,
even when I close my eyes,
my heart,
to their want,
their beauty,
their love.

You stay, full of mercy,
forgiving me,
offering me
a heart broken open
capable of learning
from you
to live love for others.

You stay with me
even when I turn away,
walk away
from you,
even when this
prodigal child
rejects Joy itself,
spurning
the Love of Heaven.

You stay,
pursuing me
with love's pure longing,
calling me back
to myself,
to all others,
to you,
hounding me Home.

For I am convinced that neither death nor life,
neither angels nor demons, neither the present nor the future,
nor any powers, neither height nor depth,
nor anything else in all creation,
will be able to separate us
from the love of God that is in Christ Jesus our Lord.

Romans 8:38-39

With You

You are here, now,
asking me to remain
with you.

But my mind travels far,
revisiting, inventing,
regretting, resenting,
worrying, controlling,
without you.

Help me return
to this moment
where you live with me.
Teach me to anchor
myself
to you.

May I awaken
to morning's new light
and to you.

May I cherish the gift
of water
refreshing my face
and you.

May I be present
to preparing
first foods of the day
and to you.

May I rejoice over
the blessed convergence
of provisions,
allowing me
to drive to the day's
labor of love,
and you.

May the rush of grace
filling each moment
take my breath away
and cause me to say
"yes," and "thank you,"
again and again
to you.

Remain in me, as I also remain in you.

John 15:4

It Is Good

"It is good
that I am leaving you."
You said these words
to your dear friends
soon to know
heart muscles
ripped raw,
lungs refusing to fill,
all sight taken from them
in grief's moonless night.

I have not known you
like they did.
I never stood in the shade
at the edge of an olive
grove and listened as the
song of your strong, sure
love rose up from the
depths of you,
kissed the wind and
set off some wild hope.

I never fell down in the
desert dirt to hold your
dusty feet, and weep my
gratitude, or took bread
from your hand,
broken and blessed,
and felt it quiet
my hunger.

But I know what it is
to ache for you to be
right-here-now-close,
so I can hear,
touch,
hold
and receive you.

"It is good for me
to leave," you said,
"because I will
come to you and
live closer than
your heart ripped open,
nearer than
the air pressing
against your lungs,
more satisfying than the
bread I once blessed and
broke."

"It is good
that I leave,
so I can come
so much closer.
And stay."

But very truly I tell you, it is for your good that I am going away.
Unless I go away, the Advocate will not come to you;
but if I go, I will send him to you.

John 16:7

Blessed Beauty

You rained colored confetti
from great maples and oaks
sending the playful display forth
with one slight whisper
to float, spin, fall,
lazying down to bless us.

You showed us ancient vines
which long ago reached up
to grow day after day,
into an embrace, entwining their
majestic host, parasites
drawing life, while holding fast.

You drew us down a path
laced with screaming red,
each leaf, having let go
of the only life it knew
to offer up stunning gifts
of grace and beauty.

You slowed us,
hushed us,
by the wide blue-grey river
moving patiently, quietly,
faithfully in one direction,
flowing gently home.

The whole earth is filled with awe at your wonders;
where morning dawns, where evening fades,
you call forth songs of joy.

Psalm 65:8

Altar of Praise

Here, by the cold river's edge,
I am gathering rocks
of substance,
before the great crossing,
to build an altar of praise to you.

These rocks will cry out
songs of thanksgiving
in gratitude
for your tender mercies,
and faithful, powerful love.

Rocks of remembrance,
piled up, a tumbling tower
meant to mark the wonder
of this one small life
you pulled from the mire
and mercifully set free.

As I wrap arms around each rock,
lift, carry and find it a home
in this crude pillar,
I am remembering you, recounting
with each rock, yet another time
you wrapped arms around me,
lifted, carried and made a place
for me, building a life
where I could dwell with you.

Build there an altar to the LORD your God, an altar of stones.

Deuteronomy 27:5

Receiving

"You gave it me!?"
"You gave it me!? Tanks!"

Two years old, opening gifts
from under the Christmas tree.

Throwing his arms around us,
his whole weight into us.

Responding to each gift
in gratitude's full joy.

Receiving. Free of worry
or shame or hesitation.

Receiving fully, the gift,
the giver, the love.

Giving back in the same
moment as he took it all in.

Fully, spontaneously giving himself,
his glee, his responding love.

Free me, I pray, to be
this child today.

Free me to say all day,
"You gave it me!?"

"You gave it me!?
Tanks! Tanks!"

Give thanks to the LORD, for he is good; his love endures forever.

Psalm 107:1

Brilliant Dying

Lord,
they say
the leaves are
dying.
But how can
this be what dying
looks like?
Glorious brilliance
pixelating the deep
green forests
with shimmering
sunshine?
Is it dying
that causes them
to sing out
such beauty?
Or is it a life time,
however brief,
of bathing in
light?
Can our dying
be this blessed?
Our living
such pure
gift?

The Lord is God,
and he has made his light shine on us.

Psalm 118:27

Small

I love being small
tucked into your vastness,
a speck on a larger spinning speck,
one of billions upon billions
of your dancing diamonds,
all held in the largeness
of your heart.

I love being hidden, safe,
under the wing of your
great love
aware how infinitesimal
is my knowing,
resting in the thought that you,
the One who knows all,
knows me.

I love being creature
of your making,
Creator of all,
carrying a glint
of your glory,
woven wondrously
with earth's dust,
finite, dependent,
designed to walk
joyfully, humbly
with you.

Great is the Lord and most worthy of praise;
his greatness no one can fathom.

Psalm 145:3

Soaring

We soared
through grand canyons
of clouds,
thirty thousand feet
above tobacco fields
profiteering in death,
above the capitol's
hostile divides,
above wall street's
gambling greed.
We soared
between billowing boulders
of cloud cliffs,
forming rocky mountains
in the sky,
weaving deep chasms
of dazzling white,
through which to
tilt great wings and fly.
A group practice run
of our someday final soaring
up and away
from earth's shadows
toward your
clear,
pure
light.

If I rise on the wings of dawn...
even there your hand will guide me,
your right hand will hold me fast.

Psalm 139: 9

Afterword

On Writing Prayers: Singing of Your Healing Love

This mute child
   finds a voice.
This questioning believer
   searches for
   the Heart of the matter.
This trauma frozen mind
   opens to you,
   the great Flow,
   and is carried
   in your sure,
   strong arms of Love
   to places unknown,
   unexpected,
   unimagined.
This reluctant witness
   surrenders ego,
   making room
   for you,
   the Author of Life
   to come.
This lonely soul finds
community
   in confession of
   pride and pain.

This shame filled heart,
   longing to hide,
   finds grace to expose
   the brokenness.
This soul
   bursting wonder,
   gasping gratitude,
   sings unfolding stories
   of your healing love.
This woman,
   still child,
   so loved,
   takes joy in sharing
   a crust of hope,
   feeding children,
   young and old,
   on you,
   Bread of everlasting
   Love.

You turned my wailing into dancing,
you removed my sackcloth and clothed me with joy,
that my heart many sing to you and not be silent.
O Lord, my God, I will give you thanks forever.

Psalm 30: 11-12

For other books by

Juanita Ryan

visit

juanitaryan.com

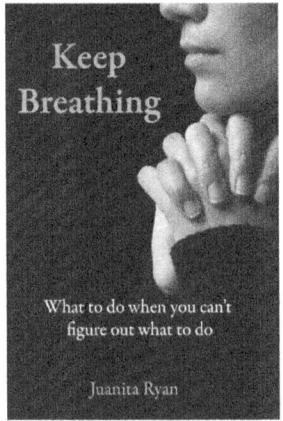

Made in the USA
Monee, IL
04 February 2025

11564194R00046